The Medieval World

Medieval

Myths, Legends, and Songs

Donna Trembinski

Crabtree Publishing Company
www.crabtreebooks.com

Crabtree Publishing Company

www.crabtreebooks.com

Coordinating editor: Ellen Rodger

Series editor: Carrie Gleason

Project editor: Rachel Eagen

Designer and production coordinator: Rosie Gowsell

Production assistant: Samara Parent

Scanning technician: Arlene Arch-Wilson

Art director: Rob MacGregor

Project development, editing, photo editing, and layout:
First Folio Resource Group, Inc.: Tom Dart, Greg Duhaney,
Sarah Gleadow, Debbie Smith

Photo research: Maria DeCambra

Photographs: Archivo Iconografico, S.A./Corbis: cover, p. 13;
Art Archive/Abbey of Novacella or Neustift/Dagli Orti: p. 12;
Art Archive/Bibliothèque de l'Arsenal Paris/Marc Charmet:
p.15; Art Archive/Bibliothèque Universitaire de Médecine,
Montpellier/Dagli Orti: p. 7 (left); Art Archive/Bodleian
Library Oxford/Auct D inf. 2 11 folio 59v: p. 28; Art Archive/
British Library: p. 5, p. 21 (left); Art Archive/ Collegio del Cambio
Perugia/Dagli Orti: title page; Art Archive/Musée Thomas
Dobrée Nantes/Dagli Orti: p. 9; Art Archive/University Library
Heidelberg/Dagli Orti: p. 7 (right); Art Archive/Victoria and
Albert Museum London/Eileen Tweedy: p. 25; Peter Barritt/
Alamy: p. 31 (right); Bibliothèque de L'Arsenal, Paris, Archives
Charmet/Bridgeman Art Library: p. 18; Bibliothèque Nationale/
Français 112(1) fol 245v: p. 19 (bottom);Bibliothèque Nationale,

Paris/Bridgeman Art Library: p. 23; Bildarchiv Preussischer
Kulturbesitz/Art Resource, NY: p. 21 (right); British Library/
Add. 24189 f. 4v: p. 22; British Library/Royal 10 E. IV f. 58: p. 6
(bottom); Gianni Dagli Orti/Corbis: p. 14; Fitzwilliam Museum,
University of Cambridge, UK/Bridgeman Art Library: p. 11 (top);
Giraudon/Art Resource, NY: p. 6 (top), p. 30 (bottom); Granger
Collection, New York: p. 8; HIP/ Art Resource, NY: p. 17; Mary
Evans Picture Library: p. 24; Musée National du Moyen Âge et
des Thermes de Cluny/Bridgeman Art Library: p. 10; National
Gallery of Victoria, Melbourne, Felton Bequest/Bridgeman Art
Library: p. 31 (left); Private Collection/Bridgeman Art Library:
p. 20; Royalty-Free/Corbis: p. 19 (top); Rue des Archives/
The Granger Collection, New York: p. 11 (bottom); Scala
Art Resource, NY: p. 16; Walters Art Museum, Baltimore/
Bridgeman Art Library: p. 30 (top)

Illustrations: Jeff Crosby: p. 29; Katherine Kantor: flags, title page
(border), copyright page (bottom); Alexei Mezentsev: pp. 26–27;
Margaret Amy Salter: borders, title page (illuminated letter),
copyright page (top), contents page (all), p. 4 (timeline, feudal
pyramid), p. 5 (map), p. 32 (all)

Cover: The legend of *Saint George and the Dragon* was first told
in medieval Palestine, but it soon became popular throughout
Europe and western Asia.

Title page: Many medieval legends told of griffins, imaginary
creatures described as having the heads and wings of eagles
and the bodies of lions.

Crabtree Publishing Company

www.crabtreebooks.com   1-800-387-7650

Cataloging-in-Publication Data
Trembinski, Donna, 1974-
Medieval legends, songs, and myths / written by Donna Trembinski.
p. cm. -- (The medieval world)
Includes index.
ISBN-13: 978-0-7787-1359-3 (rlb)
ISBN-10: 0-7787-1359-8 (rlb)
ISBN-13: 978-0-7787-1391-3 (pbk)
ISBN-10: 0-7787-1391-1 (pbk)

 1. Tales, Medieval--Juvenile literature. 2. Civilization, Medieval--
Juvenile literature. 3. Folklore--Europe--Juvenile literature.
I. Title. II. Series.

GR78.T74 2005
398.2'094--dc22

2005019029
LC

**Published in
the United States**
PMB 16A
350 Fifth Ave.,
Suite 3308
New York, NY
10118

**Published
in Canada**
616 Welland Ave.
St. Catharines
Ontario, Canada
L2M 5V6

**Published in the
United Kingdom**
73 Lime Walk
Headington
Oxford
OX37AD
United Kingdom

**Published
in Australia**
386 Mt. Alexander Rd.
Ascot Vale (Melbourne)
VIC 3032

Table of Contents

Medieval Stories

In western Europe, the time between 500 A.D. and 1500 A.D. was called the Middle Ages, or medieval period. During this time, society was ruled by wealthy lords, including kings and great nobles.

The lords owned all the land, but they granted large areas, called manors, to their most loyal supporters. In return, the supporters promised to fight for their lords and advise them about ruling the manors.

Peasants made up about 90 percent of the population. They farmed the lord's land, growing food for his household and for their own families. In exchange, the lord protected them from invaders and other warriors who threatened to harm them and their property.

▶ *Feudalism is the system by which powerful lords, such as kings, granted land to less important lords and knights in return for their loyalty and military service.*

The story of *Beowulf* is written down by an unknown author
750

800s
Stories from *The Thousand and One Nights* are collected into one book

Legends about St. George and the dragon are first told
1100s

late 1100s
The first legends of King Arthur are written down by the French writer Chrétien de Troyes and the German author Wolfram Von Eschenbach

Legends about Robin Hood are first told
1200s

1220
Snorri Sturluson collects stories of Viking mythology in the *Prose Edda*

Stained glass windows showing Thomas Becket's murder are created for Canterbury Cathedral, in England
1250

▶ *Travelers often shared stories about saints, great warriors, mythical gods, and magical animals.*

N

ATLANTIC
OCEAN

ENGLAND

NORMANDY

NORWAY

SPAIN

HOLY
ROMAN
EMPIRE

FRANCE

HUNGARY

RUSSIA

MEDITERRANEAN SEA

AFRICA

JERUSALEM

MIDDLE
EAST

Entertainment in the Middle Ages

When medieval people were not working or caring for their families, they sang songs, recited and listened to poems, watched puppet shows and plays, and admired art. Telling and listening to stories were other popular pastimes. Professional storytellers, village elders, and family members told tales of great warriors and their battles, of love and romance, and of everyday events.

Telling Stories

Books were very expensive in the Middle Ages. Most people could not afford them and did not know how to read. Many medieval legends and myths began as stories told aloud. Over time, music was added to some tales, stories were turned into songs, and storytellers began wearing costumes and masks to add excitement to their performances.

▶ *Medieval storytellers entertained nobles at banquets with songs about the battles of great warriors and kings.*

1356
English writer John Mandeville tells of his journeys in *The Voyage and Travels of Sir John Mandeville*

French author Christine de Pizan rewrites the ancient Greek myth of Minerva and Arachne in *The Book of the City of Ladies*

1405

Storytellers

I n the Middle Ages, many professional storytellers traveled from place to place, performing for people in town markets, near churches on manors, and in nobles' castles. Often, they worked in return for food and a place to sleep. Other storytellers lived in castles, entertaining kings and important guests at feasts and other celebrations.

Minstrels

Minstrels were traveling musicians who sang and played instruments in towns and in kings' courts. The children of minstrels accompanied their parents on their travels, learning the skills of their future trade. In the later Middle Ages, guilds of minstrels were founded. Guilds were professional organizations that trained new members and ensured that they were paid fairly for their work.

Jongleurs

Like minstrels, jongleurs often traveled with their families when they went in search of work. Jongleurs had many talents. They composed and told stories, especially *fabliaux*, which were funny tales about peasants and townspeople. Jongleurs also recited poems, juggled, performed acrobatics, and played instruments.

▲ *One of the instruments minstrels played was the vielle. The vielle was an early version of the violin.*

▶ *The music of pipes and tabors, a type of medieval drum, added to the drama of acrobats performing stunts.*

Bards

Bards were the storytellers of Wales and Ireland. They studied the art of telling and writing stories and poems at special schools, sometimes for as long as seven years. They also learned to play instruments, such as drums, harps, whistles, and flutes, to accompany their songs. They sang about the great deeds of kings and queens.

Bards performed their stories from memory, so their tales changed slightly each time they were told. Bards in Wales recited their stories at competitions called *eisteddfods*. They were judged on their storytelling skills and musical talents.

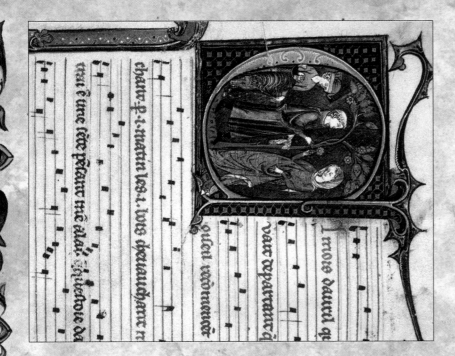

▲ *Beginning in the 1000s, medieval music was written down with notes on a staff, and the words of the song were placed underneath.*

Troubadours, Minnesingers, and Trouvères

Troubadours, minnesingers, and trouvères wrote and performed lyric poetry in the castles of great lords. Lyric poems were set to music and told tales of courtly love, in which knights performed daring deeds for the women they admired. Unlike minstrels and jongleurs, most troubadours, minnesingers, and trouvères could read and write. They recorded their compositions in songbooks, called *chansonnières* in French and *minnesang* in German.

▲ *Medieval musicians who wrote and recited poetry were called minnesingers in Germany, trouvères in northern France, and troubadours in southern France, northern Spain, and northern Italy.*

Gods in Mythology

Some of the earliest stories told in the Middle Ages were myths, or fictional tales about the heroic acts and adventures of gods and supernatural forces. These stories were entertaining, but many also taught moral lessons.

The *Eddas* of Scandinavia

The Vikings were a seafaring people from present-day Denmark, Norway, and Sweden. They told a story about Thor, who was the Viking god of war, and the serpent Jormungand.

One day, Thor went fishing with the giant Hymir. Their unusual choice of bait, an ox's head, soon attracted a strong, heavy creature to Thor's fishing line.

Thor used all his strength to reel in his catch, only to discover it was the evil serpent Jormungand. He raised his hammer to kill the monster but, before he did, the terrified Hymir cut the fishing line. Jormungand escaped unharmed.

Many years later, in a battle between all the gods and their enemies, Thor and Jormungand met again. This time, Thor defeated the serpent with his mighty hammer, called Mjolnir, or Destroyer.

▼ The Vikings wrote stories about their gods in two books known as the Eddas. One Edda is told through poetry, while the second is in prose. The tale about Thor, Hymir, and Jormungand is in the Prose Edda.

Roman Gods

The French writer Christine de Pizan retold a story about the ancient **Roman** goddess Minerva and the young girl Arachne. Arachne boasted to all who would listen that she wove the most beautiful **tapestries** in the world. This angered Minerva, the goddess of weaving and wisdom.

One day, Minerva disguised herself as an old woman, and went to visit Arachne. She asked the girl to stop boasting, but the proud Arachne refused. Instead, she challenged Minerva to a weaving competition.

Minerva wove a tapestry depicting Roman gods punishing those who challenged them. Arachne's tapestry showed Jupiter, the king of the gods, tricking people. Minerva was so angered by Arachne's tapestry that she turned the young girl into a spider so that she would spend the rest of her life weaving webs.

Celtic Mythology

The **Celts** told many myths about Finn, the god of hunting. As a boy, Finn was an **apprentice** to a great bard. While fishing one day, the bard caught a salmon named Theofis, who was said to possess all the knowledge of the world. The bard planned to eat Theofis so that he could gain the fish's knowledge.

As Finn was cooking the salmon for the bard, he burned his thumb. Finn quickly put his thumb in his mouth to cool it off. As he did so, he gained some of Theofis's knowledge. The bard realized that now only his young apprentice could gain the rest of the salmon's wisdom, so he gave Finn the fish to eat. From then on, Finn only had to put his thumb in his mouth and say magical words to possess whatever knowledge he wished.

▶ *Full of pride, Arachne refused to stop boasting about her weaving skills.*

Animal Tales

Many stories in the Middle Ages were about animals that acted like humans. Some stories, called fables, contained moral lessons. They were told by parents who wanted to teach their children how to behave properly.

Marie de France

Some of the most famous medieval fables were written by a French troubadour named Marie de France. In "The Fox and the Rooster," a fox tricked a rooster into closing his eyes and singing. While the rooster's eyes were closed, the fox snatched him up in his mouth and headed for the forest, looking forward to enjoying his stolen meal.

The rooster had his own plan. Slyly, he suggested to the fox, "Go ahead, shout as loud as you can that you have taken me and will never let me go." As soon as the fox opened his mouth to let everyone know of his good fortune, the rooster escaped. The fox was furious that he had been tricked, and cursed his decision to brag because it had cost him his dinner. The moral of the story is that fools should keep their mouths closed instead of speaking.

▲ In the Middle Ages, people told tales, painted pictures, and wove tapestries of unicorns. Unicorns are mythical horses that have one horn in the middle of their foreheads. People believed that a unicorn's horn had magical powers.

The Eagle and the Cuckoo

In the 1200s, the English **monk** Odo of Cheriton wrote a collection of fables that included "The Eagle and the Cuckoo." While flying in a forest one day, an eagle spotted a beautiful nest woven from roses. He proclaimed to his companions, "This most beautiful nest should belong to the most beautiful bird. Which one of us is that?" The cuckoo replied, "Cuc-koo." Next, the eagle asked which bird sang the best. Again, the cuckoo replied, "Cuc-koo."

Angered by the cuckoo's boasting, the eagle snapped, "You are so proud, you do not deserve this nest or any other. From now on, you will lay your eggs in the nests of other birds." The moral of the story is that it is best not to brag.

Le Roman de Renart

Le Roman de Renart is a collection of stories written in rhyme about a fox named Renart. Renart was always trying to fool other animals. In one story, Renart was trapped at the bottom of a well. He heard footsteps and called out for help. Unfortunately, the footsteps belonged to his fiercest enemy, the wolf Isengrin.

Isengrin refused to help Renart until the fox convinced him that the bottom of the well was a beautiful place with lots of food. Eager to eat his fill, Isengrin jumped into a bucket at the top of the well, while Renart hopped into a bucket at the bottom.

As Isengrin's bucket lowered into the well, Renart's rose to the top. Renart was finally free. He took one last look at Isengrin trapped at the bottom of the well, laughed, and ran away.

▶ *Bestiaries, or medieval encyclopedias, contained pictures and descriptions of eagles and other real and imaginary animals, plants, and stones.*

▼ *In Le Roman de Renart, Renart and Isengrin often competed with one another, sometimes fighting in duels, just like knights.*

Stories of Saints

L egends are stories about famous people, such as saints, kings, and warriors. Many legends are based on real people, but the stories themselves contain more fiction than fact. In the Middle Ages, the most popular stories were about saints, or Christian holy people.

Saint Catherine of Alexandria

In the 1000s, a French monk named Simon of Trier visited a **monastery** on Mount Sinai, in Egypt. The monks there showed him the bones of Saint Catherine, who had lived in Alexandria, Egypt, in the 300s A.D. Simon spread the story of Catherine's life.

When Catherine was 18 years old, the non-Christian **emperor** in Alexandria was killing Christians. Catherine decided to go to his court to discuss the teachings of Jesus Christ with him. Christians believe that Jesus was God's son.

The emperor was impressed with Catherine's words, and challenged her to **debate** with 50 wise men about whether it was better to worship the Roman gods or Jesus. Catherine was such a skilled speaker that she convinced all 50 men to become Christians. The emperor was furious, and threw Catherine into prison for 12 days. She was given no food or water, but was fed by angels who visited her.

When the emperor released Catherine, he was angry that she had not suffered in prison. He ordered that Catherine be beheaded, or have her head cut off. After she was killed, angels took her body to be buried at the monastery on Mount Sinai.

▲ The story of Saint Catherine is probably not true, but many people in the Middle Ages believed that she really did convert 50 scholars to Christianity. For this reason, the medieval Church made her a saint.

Saint George and the Dragon ▼

Saint George is believed to have been a Christian soldier who lived around 300 A.D. During the 1100s, legends developed about his courage and bravery. *Saint George and the Dragon* tells of George's battle with a fierce, fire-breathing dragon.

One day, a dragon made his nest in a spring near a village. The dragon would only let the villagers take water from the spring if they offered him a person to eat each day. A lottery was held to choose the victims and, soon, the princess's name was drawn.

When Saint George passed through the village, he heard the story of the princess, and rushed to the dragon's nest. He arrived just as the dragon was preparing to eat her. With a single stroke of his long sword, Saint George split open the dragon's head and killed it. The princess was returned to her people safe and sound.

Kings and Warriors

L egends about great kings and warriors were often based on their real deeds. Medieval storytellers added imaginary details to the tales to make them even more interesting.

Cantar de Mío Cid

The Spanish poem *Cantar de Mío Cid*, or *The Song of My Cid*, is based on the story of a real Spanish knight named Rodrigo Díaz de Vivar, who lived from 1043 to 1099. Díaz was called "El Cid," which means "the lord" in Arabic.

According to *Cantar de Mío Cid*, Díaz was a skilled warrior who fought bravely for King Alfonso of Castile, in central Spain. In spite of Díaz's devotion to Alfonso, one of Díaz's enemies convinced the king that El Cid had become too rich and powerful. Alfonso feared that El Cid would try to take over the throne, and **exiled** him from his kingdom.

Determined to win back Alfonso's favor, El Cid traveled to the south of Spain, which at the time was ruled by **Muslims**. He conquered city after city for Alfonso, gaining riches for the king. King Alfonso was truly impressed by El Cid's victories, and realized that banishing the knight had been a mistake. After many years of exile, El Cid was finally allowed to return home.

▲ El Cid always fought fiercely and honorably, making him well respected by both Christian and Muslim warriors in medieval Spain.

Charlemagne

Charlemagne ruled a people known as the Franks, whose territory included parts of present-day France, Germany, Italy, Belgium, and the Netherlands. Many legends tell of his battles, courage, and intelligence.

In the long poem *The Pilgrimage of Charlemagne*, Charlemagne and his knights traveled to Constantinople, a city in present-day Turkey. They had heard that the king, Hugh the Strong, was an even greater king than Charlemagne, and that his people enjoyed peace and great riches. They wanted to see for themselves if this was true.

When Charlemagne and his knights arrived in Constantinople, they were amazed by the beautiful city. Hugh the Strong greeted them warmly, and invited them to a banquet. After the feast, Charlemagne and his men returned to their rooms to play a game called gab, which involved making outrageous boasts about deeds they knew they could never accomplish. One knight claimed that he could destroy all of Constantinople in a single breath, while Charlemagne boasted he could make mincemeat out of any of Hugh's knights.

Hugh became enraged when he learned about his visitors' boasts, not realizing that gab was just a game. He ordered his guests to carry out their impossible tasks, which, miraculously, they did. In the end, Hugh admitted that Charlemagne was a better and stronger king. Charlemagne returned home, convinced once more that he was the greatest king in the world.

▶ In the Middle Ages, the great King Charlemagne won many battles, conquered several lands, and kept peace and order in his kingdom. Many stories were written about him and his knights.

La Chanson de Roland ▾

The *La Chanson de Roland*, or *The Song of Roland*, is a story about one of Charlemagne's knights, Roland, and his small band of soldiers. They were guarding the French army when 400,000 Muslim knights attacked. Roland and his men fought fiercely, but it was no use. Using a horn the emperor had given him, Roland signaled to Charlemagne that he needed help. By the time Charlemagne arrived, all of Roland's knights had been killed. Roland himself died shortly after.

William Wallace

William Wallace was a Scottish warrior who lived in the 1200s. He fought against the English king, Edward I, at a time when England ruled Scotland.

In a poem written by a Scottish minstrel named Blind Harry, William's wife was killed by English knights. William vowed to punish the murderers and free Scotland from English rule. Even though he knew that his small, unskilled army would not likely win against the English, he led them in attack after attack. Surprisingly, William won many battles, but in the end was captured by Edward I. William was hanged and beheaded, and his head was placed on a spike as a warning to others not to rebel.

Medieval Myths, Legends and Songs

Legends and Stories

King Arthur

I n real life, Arthur was probably a soldier who lived in the 500s A.D. In legends, he was the most famous king of medieval times.

The Sword and the Stone ▼

One day, Arthur and his adoptive father, Sir Ector, were traveling to a **tournament**, when Ector realized he had forgotten his sword. Arthur returned to the castle to retrieve it, but the door was locked.

Before the castle sat a magical sword stuck in a stone. It was said that whoever removed the sword would be made king of England. Arthur grabbed the sword. To his surprise, it came out easily.

When Ector saw the sword, he asked, "Did you pull this out on your own?" Arthur admitted that he had, and Ector led him back to the castle. Arthur replaced the sword in the stone, then Ector and his men took turns trying to pull it out. They all failed. Only Arthur could remove the sword. Arthur had passed the test, and was crowned the new king of England.

▲ Crossing the bridge was very difficult because it spanned a deep, cold river and was only as wide as two swords.

Lancelot Rescues Queen Guinevere

Chaos swept through King Arthur's court after his queen, Guinevere, was captured by an evil king. A knight named Lancelot, who had heard of Arthur's great court, was determined to rescue the queen.

Lancelot took the most dangerous route to the evil king's castle, crossing a narrow bridge made of swords. He crawled across, and cut himself many times on the knives' sharp edges. Once on the other side, Lancelot encountered the evil king and his knights, and challenged them to a duel. "If I win," Lancelot proposed, "you shall set Queen Guinevere free. If I lose, the queen shall remain with you."

The evil king noticed that Lancelot was bleeding from his journey across the bridge, and was certain that Lancelot would be too weak to win the duel. Just to be sure, he chose one of his best knights to battle Lancelot. Both knights fought well, but in the end Lancelot won. Lancelot returned Guinevere to King Arthur's court, and became one of the Knights of the Round Table, a group of King Arthur's most loyal knights.

Merlin Moves the Giant's Ring

King Arthur's uncle, Aurelius Ambrosius, ruled a kingdom in southern England. He asked the wizard Merlin to design a monument to honor the great kings of Britain. Merlin suggested that the Giant's Ring, a circle of enormous stones in Ireland, would be perfect.

When Merlin and Aurelius's knights arrived at the Giant's Ring, Merlin challenged the knights to move the stones, but no one could budge them. Laughing, Merlin loaded the stones onto a ship quicker than anyone could believe. Then, he and the knights returned to England, where Merlin rebuilt the stone circle exactly as it had been in Ireland.

Tristan

Tristan was one of the Knights of the Round Table. One day, he, his wife, and his brother-in-law became shipwrecked on an island known as the Land of Servitude. The island was ruled by the giant Nabon, who kept prisoners on his land. Tristan and his traveling companions became Nabon's newest captives.

One day, Nabon challenged Tristan to a **fencing** contest. During the long battle, Tristan thrust his sword into Nabon's heart, and the giant was killed. All the captives were saved from Nabon's terrible rule, and the Land of Servitude was renamed the Land That Tristan Freed.

► The Giant's Ring stands in southern England. Today, it is better known as Stonehenge. According to legend, the wizard Merlin moved the stones from Ireland.

► Tristan fought in many tournaments, including one against Lamorat and Drian, who were also Knights of the Round Table.

Stories of Heroes

In the Middle Ages, bards and minstrels told many tales about the deeds of great heroes. The heroes fought monsters, battled humans, and won contests.

Robin Hood

Robin Hood was an English outlaw who, with his band of followers, robbed the rich and attacked the king's representatives who were traveling through Sherwood Forest. The earliest known medieval story about Robin Hood tells how the **sheriff** of Nottingham organized a contest to find the best archer in northern England. The winner would receive a silver arrow, with the tip and feathers made of fine gold, as the prize.

Robin Hood and some of his men decided to take part in the contest. Many people shot well, but Robin was the best archer of all and won the prize. As he admired his beautiful new arrow, the sheriff's men swarmed around him and his men. The contest had been a trap designed to lure Robin and his men from hiding, so the sheriff could arrest them.

Realizing that they had been tricked, Robin and his men raised their bows and shot arrows at the sheriff's men. Their enemies shot back and wounded Little John, one of Robin's men, in the knee. Finally, Robin's men defeated the sheriff and his officers, and made their escape, with Robin carrying Little John on his back.

▲ The first legends of Robin Hood were told in the 1200s. After the Middle Ages, the outlaw became a hero, who stole from the rich to give to the poor.

Siegfried ▶

The great warrior Siegfried was one of medieval Germany's most popular heroes. His story is told in a long poem called *The Nibelungenlied*.

When Siegfried was young, he bathed in the blood of a dragon that he had killed. This made his muscles very strong and his skin so hard that no sword or spear could pierce it. The only place where Siegfried's skin remained soft was a patch on his shoulder, where a leaf fell as he bathed in the blood.

Years later, Siegfried's enemy, Hagan, tricked Siegfried's wife, Kriemhild, into telling him about the secret spot on her husband's shoulder. Determined to be rid of his enemy, he aimed an arrow at Siegfried's shoulder, and killed the great warrior. Kriemhild, angry at having been tricked and saddened by the loss of her husband, took revenge by using Siegfried's favorite sword to chop off Hagan's head.

▶ *Beowulf was written down around 750 A.D., but it was believed to have been told by bards many years before.*

Beowulf

Beowulf was one of the first poems written in an early form of English called Old English. In *Beowulf*, a monster named Grendel was killing men in the kingdom of King Hrothgar. Beowulf, who was said to be the strongest man alive, traveled to the kingdom, where he attacked and killed the beast.

That night, Grendel's mother came to Hrothgar's castle seeking revenge. She could not find Beowulf, but carried off one of the king's men instead. Beowulf heard of the attack, and tracked Grendel's mother to her cave. At first, he tried to kill her with his sword, but it would not cut through her skin. Then, he tried to kill her with his bare hands; but even he was not strong enough. Once more, Beowulf took up his sword. This time, with the help of God, he stabbed Grendel's mother in the neck and killed her. The kingdom was finally safe.

Tales of Travel

People in the Middle Ages did not usually travel far from their homes. Those who did often wrote about the things they saw and did in other parts of the world. Their stories entertained others, and taught those who did not leave their towns and villages about faraway places.

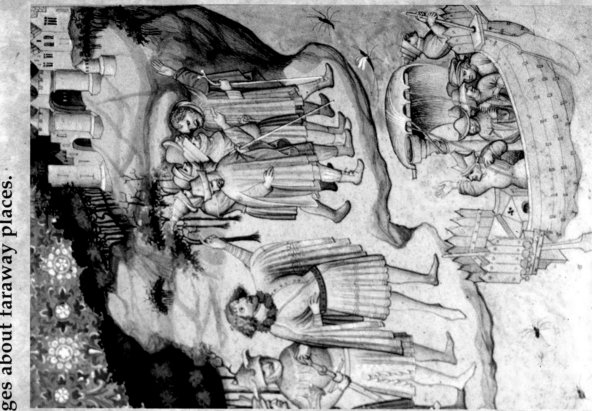

▲ John Mandeville met peasants, townspeople, knights, and lords traveling along some of the same routes that he traveled. They were on pilgrimages, or journeys to places of religious importance.

Sir John Mandeville

In the 1300s, a knight from England named Sir John Mandeville wrote a book about his travels around the world, called *The Voyage and Travels of Sir John Mandeville*. Many of the tales in his book were imaginary.

John Mandeville wrote that he met people during his travels who had no heads and whose eyes were on their shoulders. He witnessed runners who were faster than anyone he had ever seen because they had hooves instead of feet. He saw great beasts that were half horse and half man, trees that grew honey and wine, and hens that had wool instead of feathers. He also told of snails so large that people made houses from their shells. *The Voyage and Travels of Sir John Mandeville* became one of the most popular books of the Middle Ages.

Marco Polo

Marco Polo was just 17 years old when he and his father, Nicolo, journeyed from Venice, Italy, to China in the 1200s. They spent 17 years travelling across the lands of the great ruler Kublai Khan. Several years after Marco returned to Venice, he met a writer named Rustiçello. Together, they wrote Marco's book of travels, called *Divisament dou monde*, or *Description of the World*.

One of the most wondrous sights Marco described was the city of Kin-sai, the present-day Chinese city of Hangzhou. It was made up of islands connected by 12,000 stone bridges, and was larger and had more people than any city in Europe.

In the city's market squares, merchants sold yellow and white peaches, pears that weighed more than ten pounds (4.5 kilograms), and wine made from rice. In the middle of the city was a large lake, surrounded by beautiful **temples**, gardens full of fruit trees, and palaces. The emperor's palace was the most impressive of all. It was said to contain 1,000 rooms, all painted with silver and gold. No wonder Marco called Kin-sai "the finest and noblest city in the world."

▼ *Marco Polo and his father, Nicolo, described the rivers, mountains, cities, animals, and inventions they saw during their travels across the Kublai Khan's lands.*

Around the World

Medieval Europe was not the only place where stories of gods and warriors were told. Legends and myths were common all over the world, from the animal tales of the Yoruba people of Africa, to stories of gods in China and Japan.

The Tortoise Steals Wisdom

In the Middle Ages, the Yoruba people from West Africa told a story about a tortoise who stole a calabash, a fruit that people hollowed out and used as a basket. This particular calabash belonged to the gods, and contained all the wisdom of the world. As the tortoise was running away with the calabash, he noticed a fallen tree blocking his path. He did not want to take the time to go around the tree, but could not climb over it with the calabash. Angry, the tortoise smashed the calabash, scattering the wisdom all over. According to the Yoruba, that is how wisdom came to be found in the lives of people in all corners of the earth.

How the Chinese Gods Created a Storm

In the Middle Ages in China, people told a story about how many gods worked together to create a storm. Lei King, the god of thunder, made a loud, rumbling noise. Tien-Mu, the goddess of light, used mirrors to catch the sun and create lightning. Rain was provided by Yu-Tzu, the Master of Rain. He dipped his sword into pots of water, then sprinkled the water over the earth. Yan-t'ung, the Little Boy of the Clouds, gathered all the clouds to one spot. Finally, seated on the back of her tiger, Fen-p'o p'o, or Mrs. Wind, opened her goatskin bottle and unleashed the wind. A storm was born.

▼ *According to legend, Tien-Mu, the goddess of light, was married to Lei King, the god of thunder.*

How Sunlight Was Lost and Found

When Izanagi, the creator god of Japan, retired, his three children became the rulers of the earth. Amaterasu brought daylight to the world, her brother Tsukiyomi ruled the nights, and her other brother Susanoo ruled the sea.

Amaterasu, the sun goddess, was the most important ruler. This made Susanoo so jealous that he attacked his sister's lands. Angry, Amaterasu went to live in the Cave of Darkness, leaving the world without light. The other gods devised a plan to persuade her to return. They placed a large mirror outside the cave's entrance and began to laugh and sing. Amaterasu heard the sounds of happiness, and asked from inside, "How can you be happy when it is always night?" To her surprise, the gods answered, "We are happy because we have found a goddess more lovely than you."

Curious to see who this goddess was, Amaterasu stepped forward. The gods held the mirror up in front of her. As Amaterasu moved toward her own reflection, one of the gods led her outside, while the others destroyed the cave. Sunlight returned to the land as soon as Amaterasu stepped out of the Cave of Darkness. As punishment for his jealousy, Amaterasu forbid Susanoo from ruling over the sea and sent him to live in the **underworld**.

► *When Amaterasu emerged from the Cave of Darkness, crops began to grow again, people and animals finally came out of their homes, and happiness returned to the earth.*

The Thousand and One Nights

The Thousand and One Nights is a collection of stories first written in the 800s A.D. in present-day Iraq. The stories are based on folktales from Asia that were spread by word of mouth long before they were written down.

The tales in *The Thousand and One Nights* are told by the fictional character Scheherazade, the latest bride of the cruel King Sharyar. Sharyar had killed all his previous brides the morning after their wedding so that they could never be unfaithful to him.

Scheherazade devised a plan to keep herself alive. Each night, she began telling the king a story, but she did not finish the tale until the following evening. Scheherazade's stories left Sharyar in such suspense that he kept her alive for 1,001 nights to hear how each story ended. By that time, Sharyar had fallen in love with Scheherazade and promised that he would never kill her. One of the stories that Scheherazade told was "The Gift of the Golden Bowl."

The Gift of the Golden Bowl

Once there was a man who was forced to leave town because he could not pay his **debts**. While wandering from place to place, he saw a group of men entering a house that looked like a palace. He followed them inside, hid in a corner, and watched as a servant brought out four dogs.

The dogs all wore jeweled collars and ate from bowls of pure gold. The poor man was so hungry that he wished nothing more than to share their meal. One of the dogs glanced up at the man and, seeing to notice the man's hunger, offered him some food.

When the man finished eating, the dog pushed the beautiful gold bowl toward him as if to insist that he take it. The man accepted the gift and went to the city, where he sold the bowl. He used the money he received to buy cloth, spices, and other goods, and became a merchant.

The merchant eventually became wealthy, and returned home to pay off his debts. He never forgot the reason for his fortune.

Wishing to repay the owner of the dogs for the cost of the bowl, he traveled back to the house that had looked like a palace. When he arrived, he was stunned to find the home in ruins. He asked a poor man on the street what had happened to the once beautiful home. The man explained that he had been the horse's owner, but had lost all his money.

The merchant told the man about the gold bowl the dog had given him so many years ago, and explained that he now wished to give the man a gift. To the merchant's surprise, the poor man refused. Humbly, he replied that he was not the one who had given the bowl, so he did not deserve the merchant's generosity.

27

Medieval Theater

I n the Middle Ages, people not only told and sang stories, they also acted them out. Professional actors, local townspeople, villagers, and even monks and nuns performed in many different kinds of plays.

Minstrels performed puppet plays, especially about knights fighting in tournaments or attacking castles. They also performed morality plays, which encouraged Christians to lead good lives. Guilds presented mystery plays, which told stories from the Bible, the Christian holy book. Mystery plays were often very long, lasting from sunrise to sunset.

Noah

The mystery play *Noah* was based on a centuries old story from the Bible. God told Noah to build an ark because he was going to flood the world. God then instructed Noah to gather two of every animal and place them, along with his family, in the ark so that they would survive the storm. Noah wondered how he would build the ark, but trusted that God would help him. As for Noah's wife, she thought the whole idea was crazy. "Why are you building an ark when there is no water around?" she asked her husband. "Why are you collecting all of these animals?" She refused to believe Noah's warnings about the flood. Only when the rain began to fall and Noah pleaded with her did she finally agree to board the ark.

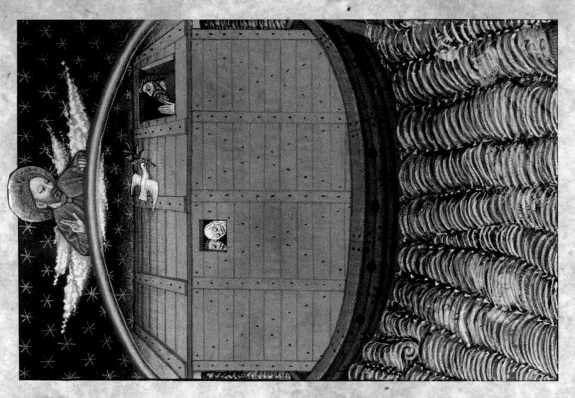

▲ *After spending 47 days on the ark, Noah sent out a dove to find signs of land. When the bird returned with an olive branch in its beak, Noah knew the flood was over.*

► *Sometimes, the scenes of mystery plays were acted out on decorated wagons, which moved around a town. At other times, the audience moved to different stations, following the scenes of the play in order.*

Maître Pierre Pathelin

In the 1300s and 1400s, a new type of play developed, called the farce. Farces poked fun at characters in the play. One of the most popular farces in France was *Maître Pierre Pathelin*.

In the farce, a lawyer named Pierre bought beautiful cloth from a merchant so that he and his wife, Guillemette, could make new clothes. He invited the merchant to come by his house that evening to collect money for the purchase.

When the merchant arrived at Pierre's home, Guillemette answered the door. She refused to pay for the cloth, claiming that her husband had been home sick and could not possibly have bought the cloth.

The next day, the merchant and Pierre met in court. Pierre was defending a shepherd accused of stealing the merchant's sheep. Seeing Pierre perfectly healthy, the merchant realized he had been tricked, and demanded that Pierre pay him.

During the trial, Pierre instructed the shepherd to answer every question by bleating like a sheep. The judge, convinced that the shepherd was a fool, found him innocent. When Pierre asked the shepherd to pay him his fee, the shepherd answered, "Baaa." "You can stop that now, just pay me!" shouted Pierre, but the shepherd only bleated in reply. In the end, the cheater Pierre Pathelin was cheated out of his rightful pay by the sly shepherd.

Stories in Art

I n the Middle Ages, paintings, stained glass windows, tapestries, and illuminated manuscripts told stories from the Bible and from the lives of saints. These works of art also told tales of famous people, mythical creatures, love, battle, and war.

Wall Hangings ▶

In the Middle Ages, woven and embroidered wall hangings decorated nobles' homes and made the rooms warmer. One of the most famous medieval wall hangings is the Bayeux Tapestry. It depicts scenes from the Battle of Hastings, which was fought in 1066 between William, the duke of Normandy, and Harold, the king of England. The wall hanging shows William and his army making weapons, preparing for battle, and killing King Harold. It was created for William's half brother, who was a bishop and a very powerful noble.

◀ *The painting Saint Sebastian Interceding for the Plague Stricken, painted by Josse Lieferinxe, tells the story of the Black Death, a plague that killed thousands of people in medieval Europe.*

Stained Glass Windows ▶

Stained glass windows are created with colored glass. They decorated many important medieval churches. In England's Canterbury Cathedral, one window tells the story of Thomas Becket, the **archbishop** of Canterbury. In the 1100s, Becket was murdered by supporters of King Henry II. Several knights had overheard the king saying he wanted the archbishop dead, and they took his words seriously. They rode to Canterbury Cathedral and killed the archbishop near the **altar** where he stood.

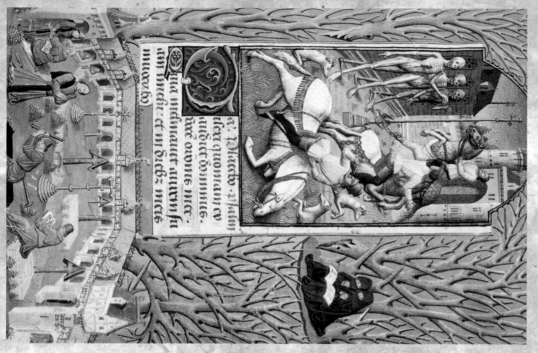

◀ Illuminated Manuscripts

Wealthy people in medieval Europe paid artists to paint small, beautiful drawings in their books. The drawings, called illuminations, were often painted with gold and silver ink, which made them shine brightly. Many illuminations were painted in Books of Hours, which contained daily prayers and stories about saints.

A very beautiful Book of Hours called *The Wharncliffe Hours* contains illuminations by a French artist known as Maître François. One illumination accompanies *The Legend of the Three Living and the Three Dead*. This legend told the story of three wealthy men who went hunting. As they set off, they were frightened by the sight of three dead men. The dead men represented themselves in the future, and came to remind the wealthy men to lead good lives so that they would go to **heaven** after they died.

Glossary

altar A table or stand used for religious ceremonies

apprentice A person learning a trade by working with someone who is more experienced

Arabic A language from Arabia

archbishop The most powerful bishop

bishop A high-ranking religious leader in the Catholic Church

Celt A person who lived in the present-day countries of the United Kingdom, and parts of France, Denmark, and Spain

Christian Belonging to the religion of Christianity. Christians believe in one God, and follow the teachings of Jesus Christ, who they believe is God's son

court The family and close followers of a king

debate To discuss or argue about a position or belief

debt Something, such as money, owed to another person

duel A fight between two people often armed with swords

embroidered Decorated with a design sewn in thread

emperor A ruler of a country or group of countries

exile To force people to leave the place where they live

fencing A sword fighting sport

heaven The place where Christians believe God lives and where good souls go after death

monastery A community where monks or nuns live and work

monk A male member of a religious community who devotes his life to prayer, work, and study

moral Relating to the idea of right and wrong

Muslim A person who follows the religion of Islam. Muslims believe in one God, called Allah, and follow the teachings of his prophet Muhammad

mythical Relating to myths, or traditional stories about heroes or supernatural beings or creatures

Normandy A region in the north of present-day France

nun A female member of a religious community who devotes her life to prayer, study, and work

outlaw A criminal who has lost all legal rights

prose Ordinary speech or writing

Roman Relating to an ancient people, based in Rome, who ruled a large empire from about 100 B.C. to 400 A.D.

saint A Christian holy person

sheriff A law enforcement officer

tapestry A woven piece of cloth hung on a wall

temple A place of worship

tournament A competition in which knights displayed their skills for an audience

underworld The world of the dead, believed to be below the world of the living

Index

1 2 3 4 5 6 7 8 9 0   Printed in the U.S.A.   2 1 0 9 8 7 6 5